GOD MADE PRAYER

by Debra K. Stuckey

illustrated by Kathy Mitter

CONCORDIA®

Publishing House
St. Louis

I can talk to God;
　　You can, too.
Mommy calls it praying;
　　It isn't hard to do.

God is always listening
    Because He loves us so.
He can hear me anytime
    And anywhere I go.

I thank Him in the morning
For making this new day.
I ask Him to go with me
When I go out to play.

When it is my mealtime
I thank Him for my food.
I know that God has given
Everything that's good.

God hears me when I whisper;
He hears me when I'm loud.
God hears me when I'm all alone
Or when I'm in a crowd.

God hears me in my sandbox;
He hears me in the car.
God hears me anywhere I go—
It may be near or far.

I tell God when I'm happy;
I tell Him when I'm sad.
Just knowing He is listening
Makes me feel so glad.

I thank God for my kitty
And all my pretty toys.
I ask Him to look after
Other girls and boys.

Now it is my bedtime;
    I need not cry or fret.
Although it's dark outside now,
    God is with me yet.

Thank You, God, for hearing me.
    I love to talk to You
Everywhere I go,
    In everything I do.